Lincolnshire Post Offices

on old picture postcards

Eric Croft

1. Garthorpe. When this photograph was taken in about 1915, Mr Leeson was postmaster, tailor and draper. Since then the post office has been at two other locations, but is now back where it started in this building and the view is almost unchanged. Card published by a London firm.

If any readers have postcards or photographs, or other information which might be useful for future publications, please contact me at 80 Yarborough Crescent, Lincoln (01522-539955)

ISBN 1 900138 10 7

Designed and Published by
Reflections of a Bygone Age,
Keyworth, Nottingham
1996

Produced and Printed by
Print Rite, School Lane,
Stadhampton, Oxford

Front cover:
Wragby. The post office decorated for the Coronation of George VI in 1937 on a postcard by Lincoln photographer Mr Frisby. The building faces the market square and apart from traffic and new traffic lights the area has changed very little in the past 60 years.

Back cover (top):
Brinkhill post office c.1905. A village scene that is almost unchanged. The post office is still here but not the Wesleyan Chapel - it has been converted into a house.
Back cover (bottom):
Saltfleet post office on a photographic card published in the late 1920's.

2. Eastoft post office on a card published by the Goole Times and posted from the village in May 1910. Another scene that has not changed a great deal, and if this photographer had stepped back a couple of paces he would have been standing outside what is the present day post office!

3. Melton Ross post office as it appeared in 1910 when Mr Hannath was the postmaster. The houses have been altered and unfortunately have lost their attractive window and door surrounds. The village no longer has a post office and the water mill has been dispensed with! This card was posted at Grimsby in July 1910.

Introduction

It is not so long ago that every village (and several hamlets) had its own Post Office and, whilst there have been a lot of closures in recent years, it is perhaps surprising how many small communities still have one. A recent trend in some small villages is the community post office, which is open only a few hours each day for basic services such as postage and pensions. This is certainly better than no post office, especially for the pensioners, and where public transport is poor or non-existent. Sometimes, local supermarkets or village shops are now incorporating the post office into their premises.

The regrettable necessity nowadays of having a protective screen around the counter has changed the character of post offices. Somehow, these seem out of place in the village shop and almost impossible to hold a conversation through!

The post office was nearly always part of the village shop or, in towns, the corner shop, but in many Lincolnshire villages the miller was also the postmaster. This was not only because as miller, and therefore very often baker, he had suitable shop premises but also because in the smaller village neither occupation on its own could provide a living.

Picture postcards were first published in Britain in 1894, but it was not until 1902, when the Post Office allowed the message to be written on the back alongside the address, that they became really popular. Both national and local publishers issued views of scenes, events and people that have given us a marvellous legacy of pictures from the Edwardian era. Where known, card publishers have been acknowledged, though many of these featured in this book were published anonymously, probably in small numbers.

In Edwardian days, there were around 20,000 post offices in Britain. In villages, the locations often moved when a postmaster/postmistress died and someone else took over in their own home. In towns or larger villages with sorting offices, a highly efficient service was delivered with up to eight collections and deliveries a day. Cards posted to local addresses would be delivered on the same day, and people could write postcards with important messages in the confident knowledge that they would be received elsewhere in Britain the following day.

An extra feature of interest on some old picture postcards is the postmark, often of the village depicted in the illustration. The postcard boom of the early part of this century helped boost the items of mail handled daily by local offices.

Eric Croft
September 1996

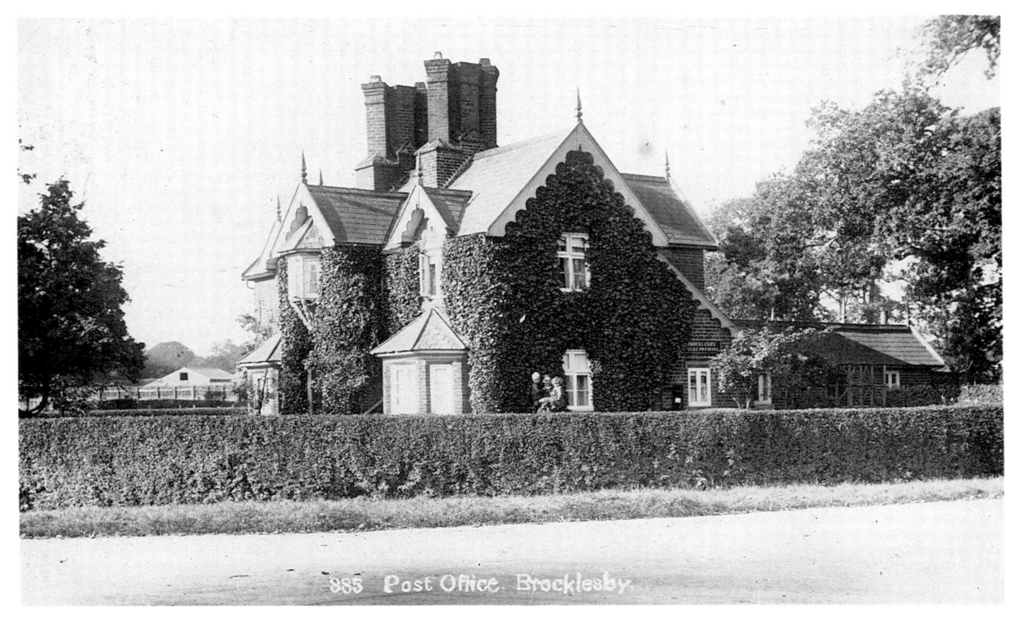

4. Brocklesby. Few villages could boast such a fine post office as this: the chimney stacks alone are a work of art! The house looks even better now, having lost its ivy, but it is no longer the post office. The postcard is undated but was probably published about 1910.

5. Barnetby post office on a card posted here in February 1908. This building was in Queen's Road but was demolished many years ago. The card was sent by Mr Cuthbert, one of the four village butchers, to a farmer at Middle Rasen asking him to send some barley!

6. Grimsby sub-post office on the corner of Victor/Wellington streets. It is still a post office but without the range of goods on sale in this picture! Card published c.1912 by J.S.Bullen of Grimsby.

7. Scartho (pronounced Scatha). This postcard is unused but believed to be c.1910. In spite of searching and asking several residents I could not locate this building which was the post office earlier this century, so presumably it has gone!

8. Humberstone. The post office has been in several locations in the village but here in about 1910 it is in Walk Road. The thatched cottage was occupied by Miss Hayes and she had to climb up a rope ladder to the bedroom! Both post office and cottage have long gone, and the area has been developed for housing. Another card by Bullen of Grimsby.

9. North Cotes post office when Mr Houlden was grocer and postmaster about 1912. The building is now a house, but all the other buildings in this scene have gone, including no fewer than four thatched houses. North Cotes is by no means a small village yet today it has no post office.

10. Caistor post office when it was situated in the market square c.1915. As far as can be seen, the only difference today is the absence of the post office sign!

11. Blyton post office on a card by Jackson & Son of Grimsby and posted at Gainsborough in 1921. This is still the post office and the 'White Hart' is still its neighbour.

12. North Somercotes. This curious building with its ornate corner pillars, fascia and immense chimney stack, is still a village shop but no longer the post office. It only housed the post office for a few years c.1915-20 which therefore gives a date to the card which was published by Jackson of Grimsby.

13. Saltfleet. Another village where the post office has been located in several houses over the years. Most of the buildings have survived. This was the premises in 1910. *(see also back cover).*

14. Theddlethorpe-All-Saints. For the postcard collector, this has everything - station, crossing gates, signal box and post office! Surely unique! The station buildings on the right and Station Villas on the left are now private houses, but everything else in this scene has gone.

15. Theddlethorpe St. Helens post office in happier times - it is now boarded up and derelict. The quaint tricycle is believed to be a Stanley Coventry lever tricycle. The card was postmarked at this post office on 20th November 1905.

16. Gainsborough. This attractive and substantial post office at the junction of North Street/Spital Terrace was built in the early years of the century but had a relatively short life as a post office, as a new one was erected next door in North Street in the late 1930s. Both buildings are still used, the latter by the Royal Mail, but the post office has moved again and now can be found in the Co-op shop! Card published by W.H.Smith in their 'Kingsway' series.

17. West Rasen. One of the few thatched post offices in the county. The card is unused and as this is still the post office and it is still thatched, it is difficult to date this photograph but it's probably from the 1930s.

18. Willingham by Stow. A busy scene outside the post office in1908. The message reads *'this is our street club feast day'.* The building is now a house but the white building near the post office (Mr Dunderale - boot maker) has long since gone. The card was posted from the village in 1908.

19. Hackthorn post office on an unused and undated postcard. This post office has not changed one iota so the photograph could have been taken almost any time in the past ninety years! In fact, it's a 1930s view.

20. West Torrington. This small village still has a post office but not this one, which was demolished some years ago, although the small cottage on the left has survived, albeit derelict. Postcard dates from the 1930s.

21. Donington on Bain post office on a card from the Cotswold Publishing Co. The post office is still here but it has lost its trees and fencing. The card was posted in 1916, when the postmaster was a Mr Theophilus Benton.

22. Tathwell post office in Edwardian times on a postcard by Roberts of Louth. The village no longer has a post office but the house is still here. Its fence has been replaced with a brick wall and it has lost the wall creepers.

23. Maltby Le Marsh. This post office has undergone some alterations and extensions since this photograph was taken about 90 years ago and the enamel signs have all gone. The main difference is, however, in the roadway, which far from being a country lane is the A1104 to Mablethorpe.

24. Torksey post office on a card by Dennis of Saxilby c.1912. The house has been altered slightly over the years and is no longer the post office.

25. Scampton. Another village where the post office has been located in several properties over the years. Apart from kerbstones and footpaths, this part of the village is almost unchanged from this view c.1906.

26. Scothern post office on a card posted from there in September 1907. The house, at the corner of Main Street and School Crescent, is no longer the post office.

27. Langworth. The village post office as it appeared on a postcard dated 1906 and published by local grocer Mr Heck. The postmaster at this time was Mr Holland, who was also the miller and whose descendants still live in the village. The combined occupations of miller and postmaster seems to have been quite common practice in the county.

28. Scamblesby post office as it appeared about 90 years ago when Mr Boyden was the postmaster and the miller. It is still the post office but the brickwork has been rendered and partly 'Tudorised'.

29. Saxilby. The postcard is not used or dated but probably c.1912. This fine Victorian house in the High Street is little changed and still stands across the road from the present post office.

LONG LIVE OUR KING AND QUEEN
POST OFFICE

30. Boston's magnificent post office (built in 1907) decorated for the coronation of King George V and Queen Mary in 1911, with postmen and other staff posing for a memento photograph of the occasion.

31. Burton by Lincoln post office on a card posted in July 1911 and addressed to Hackthorn post office *(see plate 19)*. The boards to the left of the door are displaying no fewer than 29 postcards, which would mean about one view of every house in the village!. This row of cottages is still here, but considerably altered over the years.

32.Nettleham. The village shop and post office of Mr Mansford on a postcard sent from Nettleham in 1913. The shop faced the village green but has long since gone and the site is now occupied by a modern Co-op shop which is also a post office.

33. Lincoln. This is still the main post office in Guildhall Street. The postcard was published by W.K.Morton of Lincoln and was postally used in May 1906. The post office was built in 1905 and is unchanged, except for the two arched windows on the right which were replaced with square ones many years ago.

34. Lincoln Rookery Lane sub-post office in about 1950. This junction is dominated by the new Catholic Church to the left but the post office and shops are very similar apart from the new signs. Was it child clinic time? - there are no fewer than seven mums with prams!

35. North Hykeham. The sign reads 'Hykeham Moor Post Office' and the card is postmarked 1937. The building, situated at an extremely busy cross-roads, is no longer a post office. The village has expanded so much that it now has Town status with its own Mayor, and it is difficult to imagine this area being Hykeham MOOR!

36. Heighington. This post office is a curiosity! The building is still the village post office and shop, but the front is now on the right hand end wall and it is not a stone building but red brick with green glazed tiling! It was 'turned around' many years ago but apparently the official white post office sign, seen here under Mr King's shop sign fell down only a short time ago! This card was postmarked Lincoln on 22nd December 1905.

37. Swinderby post office on an unused postcard, probably dating from about 1920. The house no longer accommodates the post office but the scene is otherwise the same today.

38. Nocton. A tranquil scene in Nocton c.1910 on a postcard published by the Cotswold Publishing Co. The village still has a post office but this one closed many years ago and is a private house. Regrettably, it is unoccupied, and looks a little derelict.

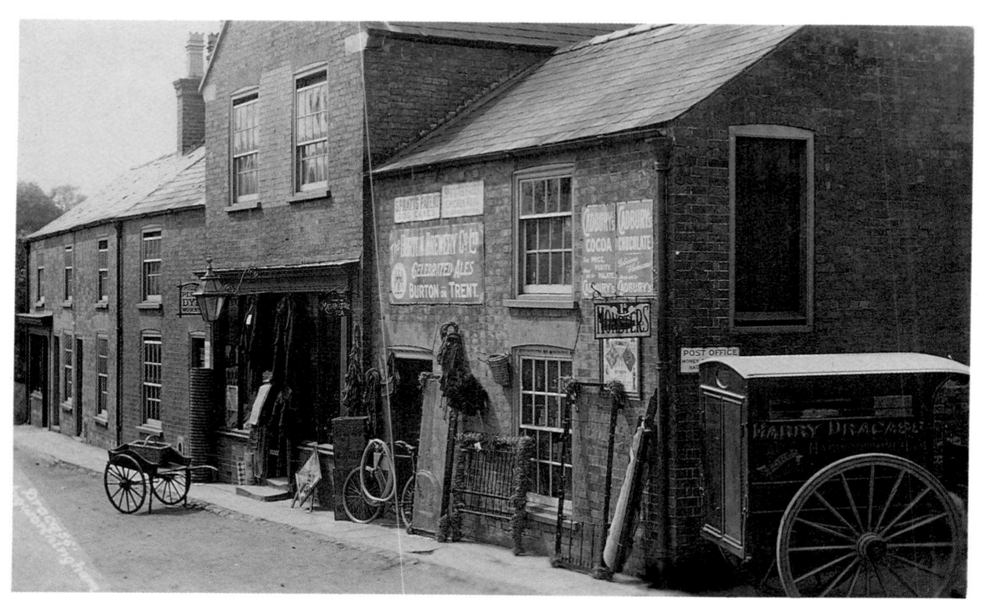

39. Hagworthingham. A magnificent card published by Mr Dracass of Hag', who was the postmaster. The goods on display or advertised include carpets, clothes, rope, bed, cycle, ales, dog and chicken food, cocoa, tea and penny monsters! The building is now two houses and appropriately named Old Post Office and Dracass Cottage!

40. Scremby village post office on a card from the early years of the century. The house is situated on the outskirts of the village, but has not been a post office for many years.

41. Chapel St Leonards. It would be almost impossible to find this building today without some local knowledge and assistance. It has gained another storey and is now in the middle of a row of shops - only the courses of light coloured bricks give it away. This photograph dates from the early years of the century, and the card was published by Harold Dodds of Boston.

42. Ingoldmells post office as it appeared perhaps in the early 1920s. The building is still the post office bit it took a little time to locate as these windows and doors have all been bricked up and the 'front' is now round the corner! A Sands 'Real Photo' series postcard.

43. Keal Cotes. This postcard was posted at Boston in 1916 but apart from the fact the building is vacant and the horse and cart have moved on, the scene is unchanged! The village still has a post office just a few yards further along the road.

44. Mareham Le Fen. Dawson's shop and post office on an undated post card but c.1910. The post office moved from here over 40 years ago and whilst the building still stands it is now unoccupied and derelict.

45. Timberland post office and the shop of Mr Houldershaw in the early 1930's. It is still the post office, although the attractive brickwork has been altered and rendered! The corrugated iron 'reading rooms' next door have also survived but I could find no trace of the 1930s Morris or the BSA three wheeler!

46. Tattershall Bridge. This small hamlet, on the opposite bank of the River Witham to Tattershall village, lost its post office about 50 years ago. This photograph is c.1910. The building looks even better today - it has two matching bays and has lost the corner entrance.

47. Welbourn post office on a card posted in 1907. The scene is very much the same today, but the post office is no longer located here. This house bears a plaque which reads *'Birthplace of Sir William Robertson 1860-1933'*. He was the only British soldier to rise through the ranks to Field Marshal.

48. Ruskington. Post Office Street - a very practical name on the card posted in 1916 and published by Peatmans the local grocers. The post office is no longer here and the road is now called Church Street. The post office is now a Chinese restaurant.

49. North Kyme. The post office is still here but the public house in the centre of the picture is now the 'Old Coach House' tea rooms. The fine horse chestnut tree has also gone. Was driving on the left optional when this photo' was taken c.1912? Another card by Jackson & Son of Grimsby.

50. Sibsey post office and stores as it appeared c.1920 and as it still appears today, except the building has lost its magnificent iron balustrade!

51. Caythorpe on a postcard posted at Grantham in January, 1908. The post office is on the right of the street about where this photographer stood. The 'Red Lion' is still in business but not the inn beyond it, which was called 'The Old Red Lion!' Part of the message on the back of the card reads *'what do you think Albert would say about a tart like the one on the other side - tell him I say she is real jam'!*.

52. Heckington High Street and post office on a card posted in 1913. Everything has stopped as usual for the photographer, including the milkman with his pony and trap. The post office is still here and little changed.

53. Great Hale (rarely Hale Magna as in the caption!). This view was difficult to locate, but I then discovered the buildings were demolished about thirty years ago! Further down the street is a public house sign but the pub (Rose & Crown) closed many years ago. The village does, however, have another inn and still has a post office. This card was posted at Heckington in August 1908.

54. Osbournby (pronounced Ozzunby). This is still the village post office and shop and still looks out on one of the largest village squares in the county. This photograph was taken c.1910 when Mr Pick was the postmaster. The cottages to the right of the post office have long since gone.

55. Allington's picturesque village post office in the early years of the century. The post office and village stores are still here but are now in a new building on the left of the house. Alas, the pump has disappeared!

DENTON POST OFFICE

56. Denton village street and post office on a card posted in 1921 but probably photographed a few years earlier. The scene is still the same, but the post office closed four years ago.

57. Stoke Rochford. This attractive and architecturally unusual post office is alas no more. I searched the village for it but to no avail and then discovered it was demolished in about 1959 for the dualling of the A1 road and was situated somewhere near what is now the central reservation! This picture would appear to date from the 1920s when Albert Parker was the postmaster.

58. Burton Coggles (coggles means the same as cobbles - smooth round stones). The village post office has not changed much since this photograph was taken in the early years of the century although it has lost the fence! The postmistress at this time was a Miss Marian Holmes.

59. Rippingale. This postcard was sent by the postmaster, Mr Laxton, to Mr Cox of Little Bytham and posted in Rippingale on 16th September 1915. The message ends *'This shows our new house, a slight improvement on the old one'*. It is almost certain this ceased to be a post office in 1926 and it has been located in at least one other house before moving to its existing premises.

60. Little Bytham post office featured on a card posted in December 1905. The building can still be found in the village albeit with some difficulty! It is no longer the post office, has been considerably extended, and has lost its thatched roof.

61. Baston. Mr Pickering was postmaster, grocer and draper when this picture was taken c.1912 and I assume this is him outside the shop. The post office is still in this building, although it has been altered with a new door and windows over the years.

62. Moulton Chapel post office on a postally used card from 1918. This post office has been converted into a house and the present day post office is a few yards to the left of the windmill. This was obviously a very busy part of the village with a post office, cycle shop, windmill and two public houses across the road (not in the picture).